T0085123

THE WORLD AROUND YOU

COUNTING AT THE STORE

by
Christianne Jones

PEBBLE
a capstone imprint

Published by Pebble, an imprint of Capstone
1710 Roe Crest Drive, North Mankato, Minnesota 56003
capstonepub.com

Copyright © 2022 by Capstone. All rights reserved. No part of this publication may be reproduced in whole or in part, or stored in a retrieval system, or transmitted in any form or by any means, electronic, mechanical, photocopying, recording, or otherwise, without written permission of the publisher.

Library of Congress Cataloging-in-Publication Data
Names: Jones, Christianne C., author. Title: Counting at the store / by Christianne Jones. Description: North Mankato : Pebble, [2022] | Series: The world around you | Audience: Ages 5-8 | Audience: Grades K-1 | Summary: "Piles of tart apples. Cans of delicious soup. Rows of crunchy carrots. The grocery store is full of tasty foods and other items to count. The interactive, rhyming text and colorful photographs will have young learners counting along with every page in this picture book"— Provided by publisher. Identifiers: LCCN 2021028245 (print) | LCCN 2021028246 (ebook) | ISBN 9781663976703 (hardcover) | ISBN 9781666326512 (paperback) | ISBN 9781666326529 (pdf) | ISBN 9781666326543 (kindle edition) Subjects: LCSH: Counting—Juvenile literature. | Grocery trade—Juvenile literature. Classification: LCC QA113 .J637 2022 (print) | LCC QA113 (ebook) | DDC 513.2/11—dc23 LC record available at https://lccn.loc.gov/2021028245 LC ebook record available at https://lccn.loc.gov/2021028246

Editorial Credits
Editor: Christianne Jones; Designer: Brann Garvey; Media Researcher: Svetlana Zhurkin; Production Specialist: Laura Manthe

Image Credits
Shutterstock: aldegonde, (pears) 29, Alexander Dashewsky, (cucumbers) 29, Boudikka, 26, Caftor, 9, Denis Pepin, (peppers) 29, Dmitry Kalinovsky, 10, Emelie Lundman, 25, genkur, 14, Iakov Filimonov, top Cover, Icatnews, 17, Ivan Semenyuk, (avocado) 29, Juice Dash, 13, kaykhoon, 19, Kevin Khoo, 21, KK Tan, 7, Kwangmoozaa, 3, LightField Studios, 6, Lotus Images, (apples) 29, MaskaRad, (oranges) 29, Michael D Edwards, (watermelon) 29, OlegD, 16, Prostock-studio, 28, Roxane 134, 24, S1001, (lemons) 29, Shebeko, (carrots) 29, Sheila Fitzgerald, 8, 15, 20, Shutter B Photo, bottom Cover, Sorapop Udomsri, top right 26, StudioPortoSabbia, 11, Tricky_Shark, 22, Ttatty, 23, TY Lim, 18, vladm, 12, WNstock, (tomatoes) 29

Special thanks to Sveta Zhurkin and Dan Nunn for their consulting work and help.

KEEP ON COUNTING

Items here. Items there.

Things to count are everywhere!

From the very top shelf down to the floor,

counting is fun at the grocery store!

NAMING NUMBERS

1 one	**2** two	**3** three	**4** four
5 five	**6** six	**7** seven	**8** eight
9 nine	**10** ten	**11** eleven	**12** twelve
13 thirteen	**14** fourteen	**15** fifteen	**16** sixteen
17 seventeen	**18** eighteen	**19** nineteen	**20** twenty

COUNTING BY TENS

10 **ten**	**20** **twenty**
30 **thirty**	**40** **forty**
50 **fifty**	**60** **sixty**
70 **seventy**	**80** **eighty**
90 **ninety**	**100** **one hundred**

1
one

Let's look around for **ONE** sweet thing.
This pineapple will make your taste buds sing!

2
two

Find **TWO** vegetables that are not green.
These purple eggplants need to be seen!

3
three

Friday night is the family's big pasta dinner.
THREE jars of sauce will make it a winner.

4
four

A pile of oranges catches your eye.
You pick **FOUR** for your mom to buy.

5
five

These **FIVE** tomatoes are round, ripe, and red.

They will go perfect with bacon and lettuce on bread.

6
six

It's time to decorate for the season of fall.
These **SIX** plump pumpkins are quite the haul!

7
seven

SEVEN ears of corn, yellow and bright, will make any meal an absolute delight!

Cabbages aren't always green and round.
These **EIGHT** purple cabbages are easily found!

9
nine

The smell of fresh baguettes can't be beat.
These **NINE** loaves will make your meal complete.

10
ten

Hearty soup warms you up in cold weather. **TEN** cans are perfect for a big get-together.

11
eleven

Buy **ELEVEN** juice boxes for the Sunday brunch.

Then mix all the flavors for a tasty punch!

12
twelve

Eggs are easy to scramble, to fry, or to bake.

With a carton of **TWELVE**, what will you make?

13
thirteen

It can be smooth or crunchy and has a nutty taste, **THIRTEEN** jars of peanut butter will never go to waste!

14
fourteen

You need to buy snacks for a growling tummy.
Those **FOURTEEN** boxes of crackers sure look yummy!

15
fifteen

It's time for the school's Read and Feed.

FIFTEEN boxes of pasta are just what you need!

16
sixteen

Grandpa will cook his one special dish.

He stocks up on **SIXTEEN** cans of tuna fish!

17
seventeen

SEVENTEEN frosted donuts for after the play.
A delicious dessert for the cast's big day!

18
eighteen

EIGHTEEN bins of fruit brighten up the aisle.
Pick your favorite fruits and make a small pile.

19

nineteen

Milk is refreshing and good for your bones,
but you don't need to take **NINETEEN** jugs home.

20
twenty

TWENTY bins of candy are a dream come true.
So many choices! Which one is for you?

There are **TEN** bananas in each bunch.
Let's count by tens before we munch!

10 ten

20 twenty

30 thirty

40 forty

50 fifty

60
sixty

70
seventy

80
eighty

90
ninety

100
one hundred

COUNTING QUIZ

1. How many lemons are in the basket?

2. How many people are in the picture?

3. How many yellow peppers do you see?

4. How many baguettes are in the basket?

5. How many items are in the basket?

The answers are on page 30.

MORE OR FEWER QUIZ

1. Are there more cucumbers or more carrots?

2. Are there fewer apples or fewer oranges?

3. Is there an equal number of avocados and tomatoes?

4. Are there more watermelons or more peppers?

5. Are there fewer pears or fewer lemons?

The answers are on page 30.

COUNTING QUIZ ANSWERS

1. There are TWO lemons in the basket.

2. There is ONE person in the picture.

3. There are SEVEN yellow peppers in the picture.

4. There are TWO baguettes in the basket.

5. There are EIGHT items in the basket.

MORE OR FEWER QUIZ ANSWERS

1. There are **FIVE** cucumbers and **NINE** carrots. There are more carrots.

2. There are **SEVEN** apples and **THREE** oranges. There are fewer oranges.

3. There are **EIGHTEEN** avocados and **EIGHTEEN** tomatoes. They are equal.

 18 = 18

4. There are **FIVE** watermelons and **FOUR** peppers. There are more watermelons.

 5 > 4

5. There are **SIX** pears and **SEVEN** lemons. There are fewer pears.

 6 < 7

LOOK FOR THE OTHER BOOKS IN THE WORLD AROUND YOU SERIES!

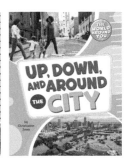

AUTHOR BIO

Christianne Jones has read about a bazillion books, written more than 70, and edited about 1,000. Christianne works as a book editor and lives in Mankato, Minnesota, with her husband and three daughters.